D1168628

# MONTH

*of*

# SUNDAYS

KATHERINE
COLLINS

First published by Honeybee Capital Press
Boston, MA 02116
ISBN: 978-1-7351493-0-1

For all of us.

*If we surrendered to earth's intelligence,*
*we could rise up rooted,*
*like trees.*
*— Rainer Maria Rilke*

*Show us belief's wide skirt*
*and the stitch that unravels fear's caul.*
*— Toni Morrison*

*Be joyful*
*though you have considered all the facts.*
*— Wendell Berry*

SPRINGTIME

# Springtime Blessing

DEAR ONES,
IT'S BEEN A LONG COLD WINTER.

WHETHER YOU ARE CELEBRATING EASTER OR PASSOVER
OR THE FIRST DAFFODIL SHOOT
OR THE MELTING OF THE FINAL ICEBERG IN THE BACKYARD,
I HOPE YOU FIND A LITTLE PATCH OF WARMTH TODAY.

TAKE A BREATH.
CLOSE YOUR EYES.
TURN YOUR FACE TO THE SUN.

REJOICE.

## ON EARNESTNESS

I recently vowed to be even more earnest, as a sort of counterweight to the meanness and cynicism that can be our collective default mode. In doing so, I was aware of the cost, that I'd sometimes feel foolish.

What surprised me was the more tender vulnerability that comes along with earnestness. When we are sincere, and motivated – not blindly so, tra-la-la, but as a conscious intention – our armor is off. We can run faster, see more clearly, breathe more freely.

But when we are not armored-up, we are also more easily bruised. One mean-spirited question, one unkind judgment, one misplaced assumption, and the earnest ones are dented a little.

It is hard not to respond to meanness with meanness, to judgment with more judgment.

Friends, there is so much we care about, and the more we care, the harder it is to show it to the world. We want to protect our caring, to wrap it up so that it stays safe.

But when our love is safe, it's also invisible.

Dear ones, whatever we love, let's show it just a little more earnestly.

The arrows will come, but we can take it.

Love is tough that way.

# ON PERSEVERANCE

Twenty years ago, I found my own little patch of ground to care for, the one that had been in my dreams all along. That first spring, I sent away for dozens of apple trees, eager to be rooted.

Imagine my dismay when my glorious orchard arrived in a little shoe box! The trees were not yet trees at all, but little pencils of tree-twigs.

The early years were not much better. The deer ate the pencil-trees to the nub every time a leaf appeared, and I did my best to weed and chase the critters away, though often unsuccessfully and sometimes with a dash of resentment.

Now, all of a sudden, or so it seems, the apple trees are spreading unruly branches over my head and I can't keep up with the pruning and picking and eating and canning.

Dear ones, we need to keep going.

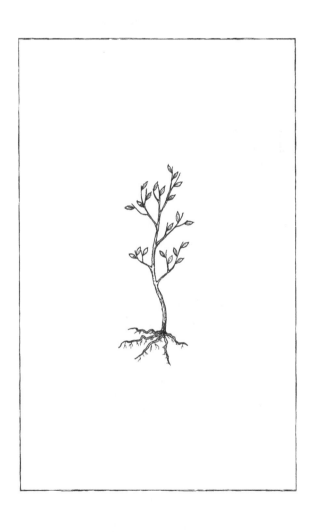

# ON JOY AND GIANT DUCKS

After a glorious wedding on Long Island, we went
to visit a duck-shaped building nearby, because
whenever you get the chance to see a building that
looks like a duck, or a car that looks like a hot dog, or
a rock that looks like a person, it's always worthwhile.

If we are lucky, life is full. There are trains to
catch and dishes to wash and seemingly endless
paperwork. If we don't watch out, it can be all chores
and no entertainment. All deadlines and no joy.

Friends, no matter how high your stack of
paperwork, it will still be there in an hour, or
tomorrow, or next year.

Let's go find a giant duck today.

## ON DREAMING

We all hold positions of trust and power – as family members, as citizens, as workers, as friends, as humans. And we all have so much to DO – the errands and projects, the bills and meetings, the mundane chores and the noble strategic plans.

Stop.
Right now.
Just for a moment.

Recall, why are we doing the doing in the first place?
Trust and power, these are precious things –
especially where they coexist.

Don't tell me what you will do.

Tell me,
What is your dream?

*As you enter positions of trust and power,*
*dream a little before you think.*
*— Toni Morrison*

## ON EDGES

I've occasionally spoken with reporters about women in finance, and especially about women in sustainable investing. I talk about the skills that are needed to translate across settings, and the opportunities that arise in developing fields. This is all accurate, but not especially poetic.

I want to talk about salt marshes and wetlands and mangroves and treelines – ecotones, edges, the places where different systems come up against one another, where both systems are present and there is also something emergent, something that is neither one nor the other.

The edges are messy. The edges are full of experimentation and invention and innovation. The edges are teeming with life.

Dear ones, if we find ourselves at the edge, let's be sure to look around, to take in the explosion of invention that happens there. And if we're safely tucked in the center – whether at work or in society or in our own families – let's wander out and explore. Let's see what's happening at the outer spaces, the ones we've been told are weird, or dangerous, or lesser.

At the edges, there is more mixing and mingling.

At the edges, there is less "normal," because we're already betwixt and between.

At the edges, difference is more welcome, and more valuable.

At the edges, amazing things can happen.

*Out on the edge you see all the kinds of things that you can't see from the center.*
*– Kurt Vonnegut*

## ON DISSOLVING

The first butterfly sighting of the season is always a source of joy. One glimpse out of the corner of my eye and I am filled with springy glee.

Of course, the outer dazzle of that first flutter is just the beginning. You probably learned about metamorphosis in school, the way that the caterpillar's own enzymes turn it into a big melted mess inside the cocoon.

Surely this gooey transformation is 100% science plus 100% miracle. And that's not even the best part!

The best part is, the imaginal discs – the bundles of cells that develop into the butterfly – they are there all along.

There inside the caterpillar as she hatches from her egg.

There as she munches her way through the garden.

There as she spins her cocoon.

Just waiting for the right time to do their thing, to give this wormy hungry creature its wings.

So, dear ones, the next time we are feeling like wormy hungry creatures, I hope we will call upon our own imaginal cells. The ones that have been here all along, waiting for conditions to be right.

True, we might need to dissolve into goo.

But then we get to fly.

# ON SHUSHING

I witnessed two new parents on the train with their baby. They gingerly settled into their seats, being sure there was no extra jostling. When the train squeaked around a curve they made sure to buffer the impact, rocking and shushing their little one. When the child looked up at them and smiled, the parents' faces were full of such pure joy that it made everyone around them smile too.

Even better, when the baby started to fuss, the joy stayed completely intact. Theirs was not a fleeting joy of a lucky happy moment, but something deeper and more essential.

Friends, let's see if we can view the fussing of the world, in big ways and small, for what it is – the cry of a most beloved child.

Let's try to smooth the bumpy ride.

Let's try to shush the noise.

Let's try to radiate the deeper love and joy that we all deserve – even when (especially when) the ride is not so smooth.

*You'll have a moonlit night if you write*
*that on the mill dam a piece of glass from a broken bottle*
*glittered like a bright little star,*
*and that the black shadow of a dog or wolf*
*rolled past like a ball.*
*– Anton Chekov*

## ON PROOF

Showing beats telling.

There's a benefit to measuring the moon, calibrating its size and brightness and place in the sky, and I'm glad to be engaged in that kind of analysis.

Still, when the ball of shadow rolls past in the moonlight, I don't want to have my face in a spreadsheet. I want to experience the evidence directly, even as I work on the abstracted data.

Dear ones, are we waiting for proof?

Are we waiting for someone to tell us that the time is right, the data is conclusive, the study is finished, the facts all confirm it, there is zero doubt, the moon is out?

Yes, let's keep questioning and analyzing and measuring and learning together.

And let's also acknowledge that sometimes, the gleam and the glitter are already there for all to see.

Sometimes we are waiting for proof of what we already know.

## ON PEONIES

I have been lucky to study with Pema Chödrön at the wonderful Omega Institute a number of times. She often describes how we can be like a fist that's closed tight, one that needs to be pried open, finger by finger. Even as the last finger is opening, the first one is starting to clamp shut again. Opening up is not a ka-pow! all-at-once process, she explains, but more of a bit by bit, back and forth kind of endeavor.

I think of this description as I regard the first peonies of the season, who clearly care not for Buddhist teachings, nor the challenges of the human spirit. The peonies are not back and forth, open and closed, bit by bit kinds of creatures.

They are ka-pow! Not blooming but exploding, beyond any idea of what should be possible or proper. To look at a peony in full bloom is to laugh out loud. What an awesome, absurd exaggeration of a flower.

Dear friends, as we try to unclench our fists, let's take the peony as proof of what is possible. It's safer when those petals are sealed up in their golf-ball buds, protected and unseen. But woah, what glory when they bust loose.

Ka-pow.

## ON SHELTER

Here's the wonderful, hopeful, loopy thing about gratitude:

Once you've experienced friendship, you want to be a friend.
Once you've been cared for, you want to care.
Once you've been sheltered, you want to shelter.

Dear ones, I know we all have experienced shelter in
life (or shelter from life) for which we are grateful,
whether from a close partner, a great novel, a dear friend,
a quiet forest, a well-worn prayer, or a kind stranger.

How can we shelter in return?

## ON FRIENDSHIP

Sometimes friendship is a welcoming pine within
a crowded forest, offering a pocket of quiet soft
ground beneath.

Sometimes friendship is a giant old oak, gnarled and
craggy and standing strong, holding a place in both
time and space.

Sometimes friendship is a clump of palms in an
unforgiving desert, a promise that comfort is within
reach, even if it is far off on the horizon.

There are so many forms of friendship, so many ways
to provide shelter.

Let's take a moment today to appreciate those who
have sheltered us.

Let's stretch our limbs to offer some in return.

*Friendship is a sheltering tree.*
*— Samuel Taylor Coleridge*

# ON POLLINATION

Would you rather be the flower or the bee?

We live in a transactional world, where exchange often comes loaded with caution and suspicion. Who is taking advantage of whom? Is the flower a fool? Is the bee a sucker?

Stop.

Look how exchange happens in the real world: most of the time, there is mutual benefit, or benefit on one side without harm on the other.

We do not live in a zero sum, winner-take-all world.

Pollination is far more common than predation.

So a better question might be,

How will we pollinate?

*For to the bee, a flower is the fountain of life;*
*And to the flower, a bee is the messenger of love.*
*— Kahlil Gibran*

## ON FLIGHT

We're all knocked down at some point,
no matter how sturdy and sure-footed we
may be.

And mostly, eventually, we rise.

It's such a relief to be up off the
ground that we might not notice at
first whether we are flying like birds
or just floating like feathers.

Dear ones, if floating is all
that's possible right now,
that's okay. Keep floating.

But as we regain our strength,
let's fly together.

Let's soar.

*One should be light like a bird,
and not like a feather.*
*— Paul Valéry*

# ON OBSERVATION

When I was studying biomimicry and natural systems,
we'd practice an elegant exercise for observation:

Zoom out, then zoom in.

Take a moment and scan a whole forest, and from
a plain swath of green some amazing patterns start
to emerge. We might see a clump of trees near a
stream that are a different species. We might notice
exactly where the trees start to give way to rock on a
mountainside.

Then zoom smaller. Choose a square foot, or a square
inch, and sit still. It might look like blank space at first,
but in a forest, nothing is blank. We might see a tiny
mite crawling across a leaf, or a minuscule scrap of
moss, astounding in its beauty.

This same exercise works for life.
Zoom out, try to consider the last
year or five or fifty in its grander
sweep. What can we see?

And zoom in, to this moment. This
one. Right here. Isn't it wonderful?
Wonder. Full.

As we zoom back and forth, I wish us the grand views
and the tiny miracles both.

# ON PRAYER

One day, my amazing mom sent me a little note
that read, "I said a prayer for you today."

This happens often, and I am
endlessly grateful every time.
What greater gift could there
possibly be than to know
that another person
is praying for you?
You don't have to be
religious to appreciate
care like that; there is
no easier on-ramp to
gratitude.

One of my favorite passages
from the wonderful Anne
Lamott says, "As it turns out, if one
person is praying for you, buckle
up. Things can happen."

Friends, as we revel in business and busy-ness,
I am holding you in my prayers.

So buckle up.

Things can happen.

## ON HOPE

In some circles it's cool to be cynical, clever to be critical. If you dare to raise a note of optimism in this crowd, you risk being branded a simpleton.

La-la-la fingers-in-my-ears optimism might well deserve this kind of dismissal. But informed hope and conscious joy are not simple endeavors at all.

It is courageous to be hopeful.
It is defiant to be joyful.

Dear ones, whatever the facts might be today, let's consider them carefully.

And then, fully aware, let's go forth.

With joy.

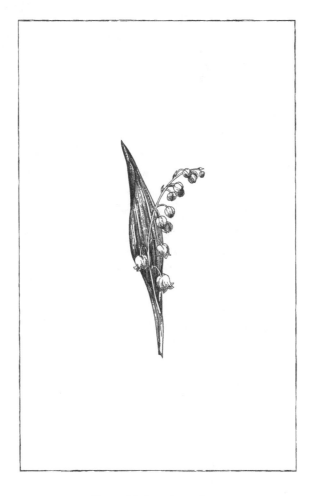

*Be joyful though you have
considered all the facts.*
*– Wendell Berry*

## ON COMPANIONSHIP

When I walked the Camino de Santiago, I met some
wonderful people, but I also spent quite a few days in
silence, speaking only to ask for water, or for a spot
in a dormitory. I was walking during the scorching
Spanish summer, so I liked to start before dawn,
setting off in the blue light that comes before the
sun. One morning I came round a bend in the road
and was nearly blinded by a huge flash of light. A
streetlight? Headlights? A lantern?

No! It was the moon, lighting up the whole valley.
You know that feeling when you see a dear friend
in an unexpected place? That's how I felt seeing the
moon that morning. Alone in the quiet, in the middle
of a deeply uncomfortable journey, I felt a little ease,
a little joy. The sun rose soon after, but knowing the
moon was still up there helped to ensure that my
solitary journey was not lonely.

More recently I was on a homebound plane, having
started off that same day in another predawn blue.

As the plane ascended, I noticed a red glowing semicircle off to the right, next to Orion, one of the very few constellations I can name. Eventually the red spot turned a bright clear white and I realized it was not a light on the wing at all, but my old friend the moon.

Most days, we are blessed to be surrounded by human bonds, by friends and family and even strangers who share connection and warmth and love. And beyond these ties, we have even more durable links.

The moon was there before I was born.
The moon has witnessed my entire life, and the lives of everyone I have ever known.
The moon will be there long after I am gone.

And for a little while, she will shine down on me, lighting the way.

SUMMER

*Summer Blessing*

WHEREVER THIS AFTERNOON FINDS YOU,
MAY YOU FIND ITS JOY AND BEAUTY.

EAT A TOMATO.
FOLLOW A DRAGONFLY.
SWING IN A HAMMOCK.
POUR A TALL GLASS.
TAKE A DEEP BREATH.
EXHALE.

THESE SUMMER DAYS ARE FEW, AND PRECIOUS.

# ON SOUSAPHONES

One summer evening, I was trying to focus on some neat new data at work, but there was a huge commotion from the street below. As the noise grew and grew, I was more and more distracted, more and more irritated.

Then, all at once, the noise merged into a glorious major chord, extra-heavy on the bass. Finally, I put the spreadsheets down and peered out the window. There in the tiny park below squeezed an entire drum & bugle corps!

Perhaps my glee is understandable to you only if you too know that five yards equals exactly eight steps, if you can debate the merits of sousaphones versus marching tubas, if you know that a shako is not a fancy breakfast smoothie.

Everyone knows how much I love spreadsheets, but they are no match for a whole herd of mellophones. This all had me wondering, how many times have I blocked out the noise, when really the noise was a killer drum line?

Dear ones, on these long and sometimes magical summer evenings, let's listen for the music in the noise.

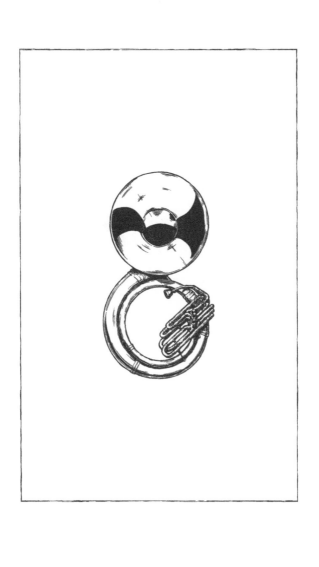

*The line on the map is not to be found*
*at the edge of the sea.*
*– Dana Meadows*

## ON MAPS

We travel for all sorts of reasons: to see new things,
to meet new people, to have new experiences. We
also travel to rediscover what we already know –
perspectives on our own homelands, on our own
families, on our own lives.

And then, a little deeper still, we travel to re-member,
to reconnect with what we know on a more essential
level. That a parent caring for a child looks the same
all the world over. That the joy of an unexpected flower
or fruit or creature can be found in any landscape.
That a nourishing meal or a kind word have the same
soothing impact regardless of ingredients or language.

The borders on our maps don't really exist.

Wherever we find ourselves today, let's take a little trip.

We don't have to fly far away to travel past the border.

## ON ENOUGH-NESS

The urgent joy of summer sometimes adds pressure, instead of pleasure. Can I see all the friends I want to see? Can I explore all the different hiking trails? Can I attend all the concerts, enjoy all the picnics? Can I read all the books?

No matter how pleasant the topic, when the question is "all?" the answer is eternally "no."

When Goethe said, "Every second is of infinite value," he did not mean, "...so you should require 3 different calendar apps to keep track of your schedule." When Franklin said, "Time is money," he did not mean, "...so be sure to maximize your billable hours."

There is never enough time. Curiously enough, this means that there is also always enough time.

Friends, may we invest in this day, knowing it is enough.

## ON PRIZES

There's a poetry contest called the Floral Games that
goes back for many centuries.

The more modern form of the Games, held in the
Basque region during the mid-1800's, offered three
main prizes.

The prize for the most patriotic poem was a sweet
briar made of gold, and for the best religious poem a
silver violet was awarded.

But the highest honor of all, for the greatest love
poem, was an actual rose.

Dear ones, what deserves our highest honor?

What is our highest prize?

## ON GLORY

One Saturday, before I had even laced up my
sneakers for a happy turtle-paced jog, Eliud Kipchoge
had run an entire marathon in less than two hours.
Afterward, he noted, "Together, when we run, we
can make this world a beautiful world. Anything
is possible."

If you look at the image as Kipchoge crosses the
finish line, what is striking is the huge group of

teammates springing along behind him, cheering and waving. Forty-one pacers took turns surrounding Kipchoge through the race, along with a host of coaches and planners and spectators.

Our narratives easily veer towards the heroic, and it's inspiring when they do. But look around the heroes, and there's always a huge supporting team.

It's easy to want to be a hero, and it's also easy to choose to be a modest contributor. But to give something your all, to be one of the very greatest on the planet in your chosen endeavor, and to still be willing to act in a supporting role... that is tougher. It is the difference between glory and honor.

This is the question. Regardless of glory, what is worthy of our total devotion?

Kipchoge is right, anything is possible.

Together we can make this world a beautiful world.

# ON WORMS

I was planting a little peach tree, and noticed that the soil was teeming with life, full of big fat worms, skinny squirmy nematodes, and lumpy white larvae, with a whole community of tiny spiders roving over the top.

Truth be told, it was a little overwhelming, all that squirming and wriggling. A small part of me was wishing for a simple scoop of potting soil, fluffy and clean and wriggle-free.

But we all know deep down: easier does not mean better. When it's in full health, soil is messy, full of creepy crawlies – and it's all that burrowing and processing that makes life possible.

Remove the mess, and you remove the miracle.

This has me wondering, in my life, what have I over-sanitized? What has been lost in the process? How can I leave room for a few creepy crawlies, for the messy discomfort that encourages new life to emerge?

With so much that we want to grow, there's only one approach that makes sense.

Embrace the mess. Celebrate the worms.

*I just happen to think that in life we need
to be a little like the farmer, who puts
back into the soil what he takes out.*
*— Paul Newman*

## ON TIME

Summer in New England is precious, precisely because it is fleeting. Sometimes this translates into a crazy-busy approach to the days – we have to go to the beach! The mountains! The concert! The picnic!

Today my Non-Urgent morning task was to watch the butterflies in the garden for ten minutes, which was enough to inspire curiosity and joy and fascination and wonder and awe.

In that ten minutes was forever.

Dear ones, wherever you are today, I hope there is a butterfly to remind you that time is fleeting.

And yet there's time enough.

*The butterfly counts not months*
*but moments, and has time enough.*
*— Rabindranath Tagore*

## ON RELIEF

On a familiar summer walk, sun blazing, my face
all pink and overheated, it suddenly dawned on
me that I was walking by a creek!  Dozens and
dozens of times I'd strolled or jogged or pedaled
along this path, admiring the water, but never once
had I gone in.

When it finally clicked, I plunged my feet into the
cool, clean, soothing water and sat still as a turtle on
a rock. Within five minutes, my walk changed from
chore to delight, from depleting to renewing.

Dear ones, what other creeks are we walking right
past, suffering while relief is in plain sight?

Wherever we are today, whatever needs soothed, I
hope we are quiet enough to hear the bubbling of
the help that's all around us.

## ON POWER

Though summer seems meant for leisure, sometimes it is also jam-packed with priorities that seem to compete. Fortunately, we have the most splendid example before us: our very own star.

The loop of energy that pulls the earth into orbit ultimately streams outward, to grow our food and light our way. These aren't three different entries on the sun's to-do list – pull, grow, light, check-check-check. It's all part of one elegant, powerful process.

Friends, as we hold all of our own personal planets in orbit this summer, look! The grapes are ripening too.

Maybe things don't need as much effort as we suppose.

Maybe we are more powerful than we think.

*The sun, with all those planets revolving around it and dependent on it, can still ripen a bunch of grapes as if it had nothing else in the universe to do.*
*— Galileo (attr.)*

## ON WISDOM

Dear friend and teacher, the wise and generous Elizabeth Lesser, introduced me to the idea of a poetry bazaar, where we wander around a garden of quotes, gathering up precious scraps of wisdom and inspiration.

The passage that leapt up into my hand was surprising, because it is so familiar. I know this verse of Corinthians by heart, but this time, a different fragment caught my ear: "Where there is knowledge, it shall fall away."

Of course, the idea that there comes a time when knowledge is useless is deeply disturbing for someone who takes such comfort in the knowable and analyze-able.

Dear ones, whatever challenges we face, let's use our minds and brains and knowledge to tackle what we can. And let's also seek out the wisdom beyond knowledge, the wisdom that is invisible because it is most familiar. The people we've known for years, the streets we walk every day, the trees that have stretched overhead for decades, the books and songs from our childhoods... let's look to them with fresh eyes.

Let's soak up all they have to offer,
the love that has been here all along.

*Love never fails.*
*But where there are prophecies, they shall fail;*
*where there be tongues, they shall cease;*
*where there is knowledge, it shall fall away...*
*and now abide faith, hope, and love, these three;*
*but the greatest of these is love.*
*– 1 Corinthians 13*

# ON HONOR

There is a lot of ugliness that is wrapped up in a false cloak of honor these days, so we need to be careful. Whether patriotism or prayer or parenting, when the word "honor" is invoked, beware. Sometimes it is a shiny wrapper, meant to distract us from an essence of fear or control or meanness.

The easiest test of truth is to ask, Where is the beloved that links to this honor? If we can see the love, the honor rings true. Indeed, it may be the work of our time to reunite honor and love.

What am I honoring with my actions, with my words, with my life?

Let's start with,

What do we love?
Who do we love?
Where do we love?

And then let's honor that – steady and deep and true.

## ON ATTENTION

Labor Day always carries with it a sense of the other kind of labor, the labor of birth.

No matter how relaxing the holiday, around the edges there is a tinge of excitement – and sometimes anxiety – about the new season that is emerging. This buzzy feeling usually leads me straight to technology, wanting to organize and respond, to rearrange files and delete emails – and there is some benefit to this, for sure. But this time I took out a piece of paper, and a pen, and I sat still until a different sort of clarity emerged.

*Attentiveness alone can rival the*
*most powerful magnifying lens.*
*– Robin Wall Kimmerer*

Dear ones, whatever we are preparing for this
weekend, let's try to set our apps aside.

Let's look at something – or someone – we love.

Look again. Closer.

Attend to what we see.

## ON COMPOST

I took a long hike with a dear friend, up through
a forest that had been consumed by fire a few
years back. It was not conventionally pretty, with
its ghost trees poking up to the sky and the newer
undergrowth just beginning to thrive. But it was
gorgeous to see all of the layers of life exposed: the
scarred elder trees that had persevered through the
flames and were puffing out new pinecones, the
grey and rotting pieces of those that had collapsed
beneath our feet, the pillars of those that had died
but not yet fallen, watching over us.

And all around – still, again – life.

The water gushed down the falls, cold and clear.
The woodpecker perched on the top of a ghost tree,
cleaning and preening, feather by feather.
The saplings stretched toward the sun, fresh and
gold-green.

For a long time, I've looked forward to beginnings,
and sincerely so. The next book, the next season, the
next trip are worthy of celebrating, piling more and
more opportunities for the richness of life on top of
what's already been experienced.

Eager for what is to come, I have not been as willing
to pause to give thanks for what has passed, for the
compost that has been made of all that has come
before, and the way that its nourishing all that is
happening now. This sounds easy enough to do, but
it requires also revisiting the pain of what has passed,
at least a little. Whether the end of blueberry season
or the end of a life, we can't get at the gratitude
without swimming through some sorrow.

Friends, as we begin all kinds of new things, let's
pause and look back. Let's thank all that has come
before – the recent and the distant, the creation and
the destruction, the joy and the sorrow.

All that makes this new moment possible.

## ON THORNS

Some ideas are easier to accept
from plants than from humans.

For example, the idea that prickly,
painful things can be beautiful and
worthy and maybe even loved.

We just need to take a little care,
leave a little room. Stop stomping
around like it's all about us.

Whatever our current habitat, let's
look out for the prickly things,
whether cactus or human.

Take a little care, and they might
become beloveds.

## ON SPECTACLES

When I finally moved into the city, the main criteria for choosing my apartment was that it had to be close to the 4th of July fireworks in Boston. For many years, that show has been my main summer ritual. I've refused wonderful invitations and rearranged all sorts of other plans to be sure I was in town for the spectacle.

One year found me in the country instead of the city for the 4th – a happy development, but for the missing fireworks. To my delight, as the sun settled beyond the horizon, I heard the familiar thwunk, whoosh, pop! And ran outside. But surrounded by hills, I couldn't see a single spark.

As I turned to go inside, from one of the tree clumps that was blocking my view, I spied a flash. A quiet one, no sound at all. Then another. And another. I was surrounded by fireflies, who have no sense of fomo at all.

Dear ones, as we search for the rare and showy fireworks high up in the sky, let's be sure not to curse the things that are in our way. They might present an even more amazing show.

AUTUMN

# Autumn Blessing

THERE COMES A MORNING
WHEN WE REACH FOR FLANNEL
AGAINST THE FIRST FROST.

THE TOPS OF THE TREES BLAZE SUDDENLY SCARLET;
THE PUMPKINS GLOW ORANGE IN THE FIELDS.

LET'S CRUNCH THROUGH THE LEAVES.
LET'S PICK FAR TOO MANY APPLES.
LET'S TAKE A LONG DEEP BREATH,
FEEL THE CHILLED AIR IN OUR LUNGS
AND THE WARM SUN ON OUR FACES.

OUR HARVEST IS HERE.
IT'S TIME TO GIVE THANKS.

# ON SPIRALS

After finishing divinity school, I walked the Camino route of St. James across northern Spain – 500 long miles. When I finally reached the cathedral in Santiago, there was a curious carving embedded in its surface.

Many cathedrals feature the alpha-omega pairing, an ancient name for God in Abrahamic religions. But at the cathedral of Santiago de Compostela, the heart of a web of pilgrimage routes that stretches throughout Europe, the objective of all of those pilgrims' steps, the characters are reversed.

Omega and alpha.
The end is the beginning.
The beginning is the end.

This notion is simultaneously joyful and exhausting. And perfect. Of course the end is the beginning – why else do we journey, if not to be changed, and to start again?

Dear ones, as our attention shifts with the turning of the seasons, one pilgrimage leading to the next,

May all of our omegas bring us seamlessly to the next alpha,

Spiraling ever upward.

*Stay right where you are.*
*Don't run away.*
*Dig in.*
– *Pete Seeger*

## ON ROOTING

I've been trying to follow a more seasonal model of work: using the winter for deep foundation-building projects, spring for sprouting up new ideas, summer for stretching out and expanding. Fall is full-on harvest mode, gathering up all that has been tended, sharing it with others, pushing to get a lot done before the quieter winter stretch is upon us.

Yet autumn is a time of planting, too. It's not for tender seeds that will burst into action, but for bigger beginnings – the sapling that needs to settle its roots before the ground freezes, the bulbs that need the dark and the cold to properly develop.

Friends, what durable roots do we want to set in the ground?

Let's be planting, even as we harvest.

Let's dig in today.

## ON EPHEMERA

Racing from a plane to rental car to highway in California, I was determined to get to Muir Woods before they closed.

That is an obviously ridiculous concept, that the woods have a closing time. Happily, the woods themselves couldn't care less about the signs at the entrance.

One step onto the path and I felt a great release. Ten more steps and I felt a prickle of tears in my eyes, to stand amongst beings that had seen so much. And when I found myself alone in the redwood cathedrals, woah.

These trees have stood through wartime and peacetime, through storms and sunshine, through human folly and human wisdom.

There is nothing I could ever bring to them that is greater than what they have already survived.

The same is true for mountains, for rivers,
for plains, for marshes... even for some buildings,
and some people.

Hand on a tree, my fury over powerpoint
fonts drained away. Feet on the earth, my
worries over basis points disappeared. Air
in my lungs, my deeper questions about
purpose and meaning floated free.

All of our work, all of our lives, are ephemeral in
the grand scheme of things. Yet if we are alert, and
a little bit lucky, some of our endeavor might help
those who come after - whether they be humans or
foxes or pines.

*One touch of nature makes the whole world kin.*
*– John Muir*

# ON REFUGE

Every once in a while, there's a passage in a book that takes my breath away.

Right in the middle of the description of the "owner men," in *The Grapes of Wrath*, there it is:

*All of them were caught in something larger than themselves. Some of them hated the mathematics that drove them, and some were afraid, and some worshiped the mathematics because it provided a refuge from thought and from feeling.*

I wanted to read on until Steinbeck made a different point, until there was another idea that did not pinch so hard, until it was time to stop reading and go on to something else.

Reading is a refuge for me, but this Steinbeck passage reminds us that there's a fine line between refuge and escape. Much as I love spreadsheets, they are meant to reflect reality, not to replace it. Much as I love indie bookstores, the wisdom they contain is meant to supplement life, not substitute for it.

Dear friends, next time we feel a pinch, let's practice letting the pinch sink in, even if it leaves a bruise.

Let's be sure our refuge is not retreat.

## ON DEWDROPS

I was out for a woodsy early
morning walk, and a tiny patch
of moss stopped me in my
tracks.  Amidst one of the driest
seasons on record in California, little
starry dewdrops swayed upon each
slender moss-stalk, sparkling forth.

Wherever we are today,
let's look up.
Look down.

Closer.

See?

A whole heaven, there for
the looking.

*Every dew-drop had a*
*whole heaven within it.*
*– Henry Wadsworth Longfellow*

## ON DEVOTION

I am lucky to have the most
wonderful mom – strong, kind,
loving, and fiercely devoted to
her children.

When I was eight years old and
said I wanted to be President,
she did not laugh. She looked me
right in the eye and said, "I will
vote for you."

Dear ones, whoever has
mothered us in our lives,
whoever has voted for us,

let's give thanks.

# ON HOLDING TIGHT

When something is amiss, almost always, my first
inclination is to try harder, to squeeze tighter. And
sometimes, when the issue is solid and tangible, that
kind of focus and determination pays off. The book
is finished, the presentation is polished, the decision
is made.

But other times, the challenge is more like jello,
squishy and squirmy and undefined, and all of that
squeezing leaves me with a handful of nothing.
Turns out you cannot schedule the flu, or engineer
a relationship, or create a heartfelt shared vision
through brute force.

Friends, what are we holding most tightly?

What if we squeezed a little less?

*The tighter you squeeze, the less you have.*
— *Thomas Merton*

## ON RE-MEMBERING

I have been showered with book-gifts over the years, a source of endless joy. The magnificent *Lost Words* from Robert MacFarlane and Jackie Morris is one of my very favorites. This book was created in response to a batch of words being swapped out of the Oxford Junior Dictionary – mostly natural creatures being replaced by techno-lingo.

What kind of fool would prefer blog to bluebell, voicemail to kingfisher, attachment to newt?

Surely there are better choices that could be made, including the choice to have a slightly longer dictionary.

I have lost some prayers I used to speak by heart, some recipes I used to cook without googling, some journeys I used to take without a map, some songs I used to play without sheet music.

Dear ones, whatever is fading from our dictionaries, could we infuse it with new life? Could we share it with a child, so that it can thrive for even longer? Could we honor it with a poem, or a painting, or a song?

Let's pick something dear and nearly forgotten today, and find a way to remember.

# ON BEAUTY

When we stand on a mountaintop, or in front of
a great painting, or in the presence of a newborn
baby, there's often a feeling of immensity, and of
connection to that grandness. Enormity. Vitality.

When faced with airbrushed ads, or glittery small
talk, or certain forms of soul-free design, the effect
is not at all grand. Instead of that joyful vastness
underneath, there's an undertow of anxious not-
enough-ness, of trying-too-hard-ness. Smallness.
Blankness.

Glamour is quick to pull us in, but beauty takes
a while. It's usually hidden behind some effort:
you have to climb the mountain, or have the long
conversation, or quiet yourself to focus on the music.
Only then is the beauty – sometimes – revealed.

A while ago, I visited the September 11 memorial
in New York for the first time. In the middle of the
plaza, there is a small pear tree that miraculously
survived 2001. It is wizened and charred near the
base, and the new growth is a little awkward and
lumpy and misshapen and miraculous.

Oh, this tree. It is not glamorous at all.

It is beautiful.

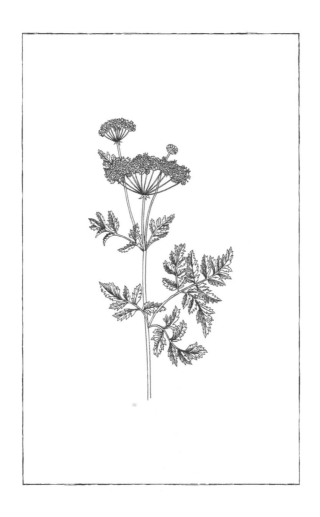

*One of the huge confusions in our times*
*is to mistake glamour for beauty.*
*– John O'Donohue*

## ON TRUTH

One of my most prized possessions is Nanny Collins' recipe box, which I have thoroughly reviewed in hopes of determining The Irish Bread Truth at long last. For decades now, our family has debated the relative merits of buttermilk versus regular milk, raisins versus currants, x-scored on top or plain.

Everyone in our family has a vivid memory that's sparked by Irish bread – it is the Collins madeleine.

For me, one bite brings me back to my great grandma Norton's table in Brooklyn, where I have been served real tea in a real teacup for the first time in my life and I'm surrounded by dozens of grownups who all seem to know me even though we've not met before.

Turns out there are seven recipes in that box, each a tiny bit different — including one from those heathens the Downeys, who apparently have no concept of a proper caraway/currant ratio. The original Norton version begins, "Nine cups of flour..."

Maybe there are many Irish Bread Truths? Maybe Truth is a personal thing? Maybe Truth is an endless quest? Maybe Nanny just wanted to keep us guessing.

Dear ones, let's be grateful for our memories, and the tastes that bring them forth – regardless of the recipe.

## ON REST

I saw my first red and gold leaves this week, even as the tomatoes are still leaping off the vines and the splashing is still loud in the lake beyond the woods. The coming turn of season has me thinking about the differences between rest and vacation, and how we jumble the two together sometimes.

Rest can be a minute or a month. It restores us, brings us back to an essential state of clarity and presence.

Vacation can sometimes be the opposite. We might find ourselves rushing for flights, tossing and turning in unfamiliar beds, preoccupied with guidebooks or dinner reservations or who brought the sunscreen. We might step on a sharp seashell or read a poignant novel that plunges us into despair instead of peace.

Friends, whether for a week or an hour or the space of a single breath, in the midst of the busyness, I wish you rest.

*Rest is the conversation between what we love to do and how we love to be.*
*– David Whyte*

*Mysteries are not necessarily miracles.*
*– Johann Wolfgang von Goethe*

# ON MIRACLES

It's true, mysteries are not necessarily miracles.

Sometimes a heart-shaped cloud is just a cloud, not a message from beyond. Sometimes the gorgeous flower growing in an unexpected place was transported by squirrels, not angels.

But the reverse is true too. Have you ever really looked at a pine cone, or considered the circulation of air through your lungs, or seen one small child comfort another? There's some awfulness in our world. But it is full of miracles too.

The leaves are turning in New England, and I know that this is a perfectly explainable scientific phenomenon. But that does not detract one scintilla from the miracle. In fact, it amplifies.

Let's look for spots where science reinforces spirit, and vice versa. Miracles need not be mysteries.

## ON STORMS

The Sisters of St. Joseph in New Orleans are turning their giant former convent property into a water garden that will be a wetlands buffer against future storms.

"What we were doing is praying for an idea that would allow this land to keep ministering," explained one of the leaders.

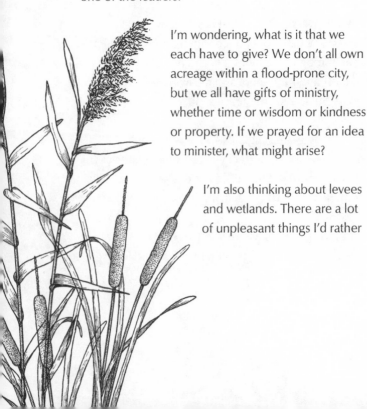

I'm wondering, what is it that we each have to give? We don't all own acreage within a flood-prone city, but we all have gifts of ministry, whether time or wisdom or kindness or property. If we prayed for an idea to minister, what might arise?

I'm also thinking about levees and wetlands. There are a lot of unpleasant things I'd rather hold at bay, building a strong barrier and avoiding them altogether. But a levee takes so much effort, and vigilance, and sometimes it catastrophically fails. What if our approach to the unwelcome parts of life looked more like a wetland, letting conditions wash over us and filter through?

We'd get a little wet, but it might hurt less.

Dear ones, let's learn from the nuns and the wetlands this week.

We can't stop the rains, but we can bring a different spirit when the clouds roll in.

## ON CLOSENESS

Distance might make the heart grow fonder, but there's something to be said for proximity, too.

Proximity is not the same as cocooning, when we just stay close to the people and places we already love. It's getting closer to the uncomfortable things (and people) that we'd just as soon avoid.

Beekeeping might provide some good lessons. To approach a hive, especially one that's out of sorts, requires steadiness and patience and love and determination. And maybe a protective hat. But once you're close, woah, you can learn so much more.

Next time we feel that "ooof, get me out of here" feeling, might we stay a little longer? Might we ask a sincere, open question? Might we observe, or listen, instead of flailing around and prompting a sting?

Oh! What we could learn!

If we practice, eventually we might even be able to live in real partnership. We could leave the veils at home.

## ON DURATION

I spend a lot of weekdays considering investment duration, but friendships that go the distance are truly precious. To witness someone's life unfold, to see how it cris-crosses with your own, to know a person – and to be known – across time and space and circumstance... what a terrific gift.

Some friends are steady like mountains, quiet presences that endure. Some are like rocks thrown in a pond, splashy at times, yet with ripples that extend ever outward. Some are the very ground beneath us, the places that hold us up when we are broken and exhausted.

Dear ones, wherever we find ourselves today, let's take a moment to appreciate the people in our lives with staying power – rare, and vital, and essential.

True gold.

> *Make new friends, but keep the old*
> *One is silver and the other gold.*
> *– Brownie Girl Scout song, best sung in a round,*
> *by a chorus of very cute kids wearing beanies.*

## ON COMPOUNDING

888.

That's how many months of marriage my
grandparents enjoyed – 74 years!

Thinking of them is a terrifically tangible way for me
to think about longer-term time horizons.

What investments could we make to optimize an
888-month time horizon, or 8888 months, the lifetimes
of generations to come?

We could celebrate more.
We could save more – and not just money.
We could plant more trees.
We could spend more time with children, young and old.

Compounding interest, in its highest form.

## ON COURAGE

When we're perplexed, it helps to dig down in
the roots – and this goes for language, too. One
of my favorite lessons from divinity school was
a casual conversation about the root words for
Bravery and Courage.

The root for brave is linked to a front or face.
Bravery is a kind of armor, a game face, an outer
shell of strength.

The root for courage is coeur, the French word
for heart. It is strength from within, strength of
the heart. A totally different root.

It is brave to speak with conviction. It is courageous to say, "I don't know."

It is brave to quietly persevere. It is courageous to speak up.

It is brave to forge a new path. It is courageous to continue when no one's cheering you on.

It is brave to be busy. It is courageous to be still.

It is brave to shout. It is courageous to listen.

It is brave to hold back tears. It is courageous to let them flow.

Dear friends, we have been trained to be endlessly brave.

Let's train for courage now.

## ON THANKSGIVING

One of my favorite meditations is to sketch a spiral of thankfulness. Pick an object near you, like a coffee cup. First, give thanks for the object itself, how it provides utility and improves your day.

Now take one spiral out. Think of how that object came to be before you right now. The person who bought it, the store that sold it, the driver who carried it, the potter who crafted it...

Now spiral a bit further, to the clay that was dug, the minerals for the glazing... just a few layers of exploration, and we are already realizing the cup is not an "it," it's part of the living earth.

And if we're thankful for the earth, we are thankful for the stars, for the galactic explosions that formed our planet. That boring coffee cup, brought to me through a giant web of human cooperation, is a pile of stardust.

With just one or two spirals it is easy to be overwhelmed by good fortune, by the beauty and power and connection of the universe.

It's no coincidence that we have a holiday for thankfulness as the days are getting darker. The gratitude, along with the harvest, can fill us up for the long winter ahead.

In the dark and in the cold, we are surrounded by stars.

WINTER

*Winter Blessing*

WHEN A MOTHER REDWOOD FALLS,
FROM HER ROOTS A CIRCLE OF SAPLINGS SPRINGS UP.

AS THE FAIRY RING GROWS,
IT BECOMES A CATHEDRAL.
BUILT ON THE ROOTS
THAT OUTLIVE ANY ONE TREE.

DEAR ONES, MAY OUR ROOTS BE STRENGTHENED
ALL THROUGH THESE SEASONS.
HOLDING US, THOSE WHO ARE HERE NOW,
THOSE WHO HAVE COME BEFORE,
AND THOSE WHO ARE YET TO APPEAR.

MAY WE BE LINKED ABOVE GROUND AND BELOW.

AS THE DAYLIGHT FADES AND THE FIRE GLOWS,
MAY OUR ROOTS HOLD FAST.

CATHEDRALS ABOVE, CATHEDRALS BELOW.

## ON ECOTONES

The solstice is approaching, as the Northern hemisphere of earth tips back towards the light. It's a time of betwixt and between – we're ending one season, and one calendar year, and there's often a big fuss to clearly mark the end of one thing and the beginning of another.

But in the in-between, in the tipping spots, lots of good stuff lives. In ecotones, like salt marshes or mangroves, we see a great buzz of biodiversity and rapid evolution and near-miraculous transformation. Salt water that turns to fresh! Creatures that live on both land and sea!

It's uncomfortable, being in that in-between space, where we've left one familiar spot but have not yet arrived at the next. To avoid that queasy, floaty feeling, usually we do what we can to hurry through the transition, back to firmer ground. Is it December or January? Are we on land or at sea?

Dear friends, let's pause here, right on the edge the light, for just a moment. Take a deep breath. Feel the turning. Stretch out, and touch the edges on either side.

Float in a patch of in-between.

See what might be transformed.

# ON DAYBREAK

One of the best things about long winter nights is the chance to curl up with a book-friend. And just like human friends, once in a while a book tells me something that sticks for a very long time indeed.

Years ago, , I was gifted a lovely little book called *The Unfinished Angel*. Some of the story is now hazy to me, but I do recall a scene where daybreak is greeted. "Lo, the pinking of the dawn!"

I loved how "pinking" was both verb and noun. I loved how this phrase was simultaneously grandiose and funny. I loved how the very next day, I witnessed the pinking of the dawn myself, and it was perfect.

Summer sunsets are warm and glorious, celebrations of the day that is passing.

Winter sunrises are the inverse - gentle and comforting, celebrations of that the day is just arriving.

On the solstice morning, we've tipped into the light. The day is just arriving.

Lo! The pinking of the dawn!

## ON PLAY

One reason winter can seem so long is that its shorter days appear to contain less time for play. When we're outside in the summer, we naturally have more chances to skip stones on a pond, to ride a bike without tracking the rpm's, to stroll along marveling at the sunset.

When I have time with my two favorite small people, it is a great reminder that we can play anywhere, anytime. Walking down a sidewalk? We can test how long we can gallop like a horse. Bored, with just a scrap of paper at hand? We can see how many words can be spelled with just 6 letters. Loafing on the sofa? We can tell stories from our own family lore, embellishing as we go.

This goofy together-time reminds me that time spent not-working is not the same as play. In fact, my own calendar is very poorly categorized: a new puzzle to analyze at the office is way more fun for me than time on a soulless treadmill at the gym. The neat Econ 101 divisions of "work" and "leisure" don't match up.

As we settle in for Monday's appointments and Thursday's spreadsheets, let's be sure our work includes some play. And as we clock miles on the treadmill and hours driving to the ski slopes, let's be sure our leisure includes some real fun.

## ON DARKNESS

In the darkest of the dark season in Boston, it is a glow-y joy to walk down Commonwealth Avenue, where the trees are all wrapped in fairy lights. Surrounded by the tunnel of their branches, the blackness seems comforting instead of foreboding, and the city seems welcoming instead of hostile.

When the tradition began, the lights were pretty, but limited. However, an interesting effect has emerged in the past couple of years: one by one, the buildings that line the outer edge of the avenue have added their own lights, in a similar style. And if you turn down some side streets, the same thing has happened. It's not everywhere, but it's a lot – and it's more than ever would have happened without the shining example of that middle stretch along the mall. There's a contagion of light!

Dear ones, we are all trying so hard.
Sometimes it's possible to blaze forth
with our own brilliance, and sometimes all
we've got is a pale flicker. Sometimes we
are alone on an endless walk, in the dark
and the cold. So when we are able, if we
muster up even a little spark, it's not only
for ourselves, it's for all who are walking
along with us.

This is a dark season for many.

Every season is a dark season for many.

So when we can, let's add our light. Just
one lumen, just one candle... it all adds up.

It's contagious.

# ON MAKING WAVES

One of the great joys of beekeeping is the chance to witness cooperative behavior in many forms. But bees are also pretty extraordinary as individuals.

A wonderful friend sent me a research summary that explained how honeybees move in water when their wings are too wet to fly. Some insects paddle, some use their legs, and some just float, but honeybees tilt their wings to create tiny waves on the water's surface, and the waves then propel them forward.

We stand on the edge of a new year, and maybe a new era. Many days we'll be waterlogged, unable to take flight, and we might not be surrounded by our cooperative hive when this happens.

We can thrash around to try to gain a footing, or we can float along and hope for the best.

Friends, maybe we can do something more interesting, more beautiful.

Let's make our own waves.

## ON BASKING

On a chilly evening, there's nothing more welcome than a cozy fireside. One particular hearth I visited recently came complete with an expert fire-builder, who piled the logs into a complex and beautiful cris-crossing structure.

As the flames crackled away, it became clear that the structure was in peril, ready to collapse as the lower tiers turned to ash. A little pinprick of anxiety lodged in the back of my mind, and sure enough, just as I reached for the poker in a desperate attempt to avert disaster, the beautiful structure fell into a heap, sparks flying everywhere.

A small wave of dismay rose up – this was a minor loss, to be sure, but it had been such a perfect fire, and now it was ruined.

But as the sparks cleared, I noticed an odd development. The fire was even better than before!

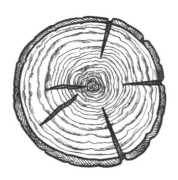

The collapse had whooshed more air in between
the logs, making the flames leap even higher,
even brighter. It was not as tidy as before, but it
sure was great.

We are all so carefully tending the fires of our lives,
poking here and there even when we know it's not
really needed. We are constantly propping things
up, adding so much fuel that there's no room for air,
checking and re-checking instead of basking in the
glow of all we've created.

This week, let's run one less errand, send one less
email, schedule one less meeting.

Let's aim to fuss just a little less, bask just a
little more.

# ON SKIDDING

As any good New Englander knows, when you start
to skid on the ice, you have to ease up, lifting off
the pedals and giving in to the direction of the skid
before gently steering away.

This takes a lot of practice, because when we start
to slide the natural impulse is to press harder, to
clutch the wheel, slam the brakes, and veer sharply
back on course.

Of course, even if you follow your drivers ed training
perfectly, sometimes you still end up spun right
'round, facing ongoing traffic with nothing but the
goodwill and skill of others to save you.

Friends, as we slide into the new year, I hope
the weather is fine, the traction is great, and the
obstacles are nonexistent.

But when we find ourselves skidding, I wish us the
ability to ease up, just for a moment, instead of
always pushing harder.

And when all else fails, I wish for alert and kind
drivers alongside us, who will gently swerve to
give us space, and maybe even stop to help us on
our way.

## ON ENDURANCE

A friend and I were trading thoughts on what we've
learned as we've gotten older. She noted,

"I no longer endure."

My first thoughts were, oh dear! Are you tired, or
weak, or incapable?

And then I thought, ohhhhh.

We are deeply trained to think that endurance is a virtue, but sometimes stopping or quitting or leaving is by far the best – and most courageous – thing to do.

We could cancel the meeting that is neither necessary nor informative. We could skip sweeping the floor that is perfectly clean already. We could stop smiling and nodding at the boorish conversation that deserves neither agreement nor tolerance.

Dear ones, what is worthy of our endurance?

*It takes courage…we have to
choose between risk and risk.
– Brother David Steindl-Rast*

# ON RISK

Whether in investing or life, we like to pretend that risk is something we can choose. But even when that's true, it's not a choice of whether, it's a choice of type.

If we choose the "risk free" option, it just means we're choosing one risk over another. A money market fund has very low risk of loss, but enormous risk of no-gains. A career spent in a risk free job might bring a guarantee of no-learning. A risk free social life comes with high chances of boredom, or loneliness.

A risk free existence might be only an existence, and not much of a life

Whatever we choose today, it will be a risk.

Let's choose the risk that's worth taking.

## ON DANCING

Some days. Some weeks. Some months... are doozies. My lizard brain is sometimes steeped in fear, circling upon itself, hyper-vigilant and waiting for further attack.

It was in this state that I attended a concert – happily, but it was a weeknight, and so I was thinking of all the other things that needed to get done once the music was over.

For the first part of the performance I was appreciative, in a sort of analytical, far-off way. Then somehow, finally, it all came rushing in. The bass was thumping in through our feet and out the tops of our heads, and the band was focused and immensely talented, and the singer was iconic and brave and generous and he was having SO MUCH FUN that we were infected and at long last we all were on our feet, dancing our butts off.

We have buckets of cold water pouring down on us daily. We are often trying to light the fire of our spirits with a single soggy match. So when we feel a little spark, it's natural that we'd sometimes think, why bother? The next deluge is coming soon.

But we are not here only to persevere. The rain is coming regardless. So when we feel a spark, our job is to protect it.

We need to fan the flames.

Friends, let's not stay seated.

Let's dance our butts off.

## ON DEFINITION

I spend most weekdays knee-deep in defining, and this is certainly worthwhile endeavor.

But for some of our biggest and best questions, defining diminishes.

Come Sunday, I'm ready for fewer spreadsheets, more poetry. Fewer calculations, more relationships. Fewer measurements, more flight.

Dear ones, as we aim to define our world, I wish us the biggest and most complete dictionaries around.

And when the most magnificent questions of all arise, I wish us time together to ponder them, in motion and undefined.

*To define means to fix,*
*and real life isn't fixed.*
*— Alan Watts*

## ON SURPRISES

In the middle of a
busy conference,
I darted outside
to get a breath of
outdoors. Immediately, I was stopped in my tracks by
the beautiful sound of birdsong, and very close by!
Sure enough, right at eye level, she was singing away
and completely undisturbed by my presence. After
a moment of taking it in, I even took a little video, so
that I could carry this glimpse of spring back to the
north with me.

There I was, communing with nature, sun on my
face, all blissed-out and one with the world, when
suddenly the bird coughed up a big orange berry,
and spat it right at my face.

Friends, if our perfect picture has a ragged edge
today, let's take the opportunity to celebrate its
surprising imperfection.

Let's bust out laughing.

Let's opt for joy.

## ON FAITH

In my home parish of St. Ignatius, where I received First Communion and counted the days until the summer carnival and played one of the Three Wise People in the Christmas pageant, some of our childhood priests have been named for actions that are about as far from holy as you can get.

A lot has been taken. A lot has been broken.
Too much.

But here's what they have not taken.

They have not taken the feeling of peace that I first found as a little toddler, visiting the quiet church on weekdays with my mom. They have not taken my regard for strong and loyal communities. They have not taken the meaning I find in devotion and prayer and ritual. It is in these corners of transcendence that my bruised faith still finds shelter.

Dear ones, it's dreadful to realize – over and over again – how many individuals and institutions will betray our trust, sometimes in unspeakable ways.

It might be impossible to ever regain that trust.

But oh, if we can, even as our trust is crushed -
Let's try to keep our faith.

*There are three signs of a hypocrite:*
*when he speaks, he speaks lies;*
*when he makes a promise, he breaks it;*
*and when he is trusted, he is treacherous.*
— *Prophet Muhammad*

*To pay attention, this is our*
*endless and proper work.*
*— Mary Oliver*

# ON INVESTING

It's a funny phrase, and apt: we don't make attention, or do attention, we pay attention. It does often feel like a cost.

When we are called to pay attention, it's because our focus is elsewhere. Pay attention to the algebra lesson, because we are daydreaming out the spring window. Pay attention to our calendar, because we are already late for the next meeting.

These smaller calls to attention can be irritating, because they live on the surface. But when we pay attention to paying attention, some bigger calls arise.

We can pay attention to the question that we're too quick to answer, because it pokes at an overwhelming topic that we'd rather make tidy.

We can pay attention to the friend who is not quite herself, because something unspoken is pulling her off-center.

We can pay attention to the first flower on the first branch that is finally blooming in the spring, knowing that it harkens so much glory to come.

This attention that we're paying, it's not a cost.

It's an investment.

## ON WAITING

When it was so cold we were counting our degrees on one hand, I tromped through the snowdrifts to bring some witch hazel twigs indoors. For a few weeks, I had a jar of bare branches sitting on my windowsill.

Nothing brightens up a new apartment like a bundle of sticks!

Every morning, I sipped my tea and checked on the witch hazel, cheering it on –

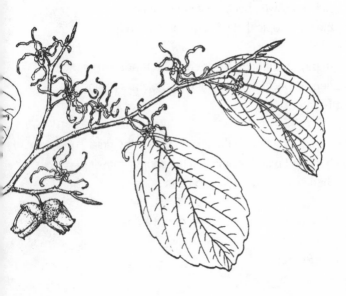

but day after day, nothing. It was clear the branches were never going to bloom; I'd cut them too soon. Finally, I gave up and bundled the twigs together for the trash can.

And there it was.

One teeny tiny scrawny bloom, just starting to uncurl. And then, more!

Dear friends, let's not give up on springtime, whether in a jar or in our hearts.

Hold on.

## ON PERSPECTIVE

A few years back, the Cassini spacecraft beamed back its final images from Saturn. One image after another shows a sea of dots – some stars, some planets, a grand and detailed sweep of our galaxy. Earth is a teeny tiny glowing pixel, a drop in the cosmic ocean.

See that little speck?

That's us.

All of us.

Our joys and our sorrows. Our most glorious achievements and our most horrible mistakes. All the people we've ever loved. All of our stories – the truths and the fictions. All of the elephants and kittens and spiders and sea stars and creatures of the deep we have yet to meet. All of the sand dunes and mountaintops. All of the rivers and oceans. The land and the seas. The storms and the calm.

So tiny.

So immense.

Look.

# LIMINALITY

# THE IDES OF MARCH, 2020

Oh, dear friends, what a time.

This week I set up a home office and argued with a
lady in CVS who was taking the whole shelf of hand
sanitizer and watched the stock market plummet
and read so many scary headlines and it was all
perseverance and planning and analysis and fine,
okay, fine, and then on Friday night I watched people
singing across the empty streets of Italy and burst
into tears.

On Saturday, I read some Wendell Berry and took a
long walk in the woods and found a long-ago stone
wall running through the trees, one that I'd seen on
an old property map but never been able to find.

This tumult, like all tumult, reminds us of how fragile
we are. It also reminds us of what is essential, and
what we can do.

We can work together. We can help one another.
We can seek solace. We can look for the new
questions that are emerging. We can recognize the
insights that arise.

We can consult the old maps, the ones that are
nearly forgotten.

We can find the markers through the woods that are
waiting to be rediscovered.

*May we be safe.*

## MARCH 2020

We were in the middle of analyzing some news and data
when one of my colleagues made a profound observation:

*It's hard to tell what's being caused, and what's
being revealed.*


We are seeing how fragile our systems can be.

We are seeing how fragile our own well-being can be.

We are seeing how time can be both fleeting and endless.

We are seeing how many are working in care of others.

We are seeing how solace can come in word or touch,
in taste or sound, in movement or rest.

We are seeing how the unfurling of a leaf or blooming
of a bud is miraculous.


Essential elements are being revealed, like rocks at low tide.

Shhhhh.

Look.

*May we be still.*

# MARCH 2020. STILL.

*A human being is part of a whole...(yet) he experiences*
*himself as something separated from the rest –*
*a kind of optical delusion of his consciousness.*
*- Albert Einstein*

We have been steeped in uncertainty and unknowing
recently, and it's showing. My social media feed is full
of baking and hiking, and also full of suffering and
prayers and graphs. Every day I visit one particular tree,
and every day I update a spreadsheet of some of the
saddest numbers I've ever seen.

We are all searching for understanding, but there is
something more too: we are all searching for safety.
Oh how we long to think, well, it's only over there, and
then well, it's only very old people, and then well, it's
only very sick people, and then well, it's only smokers,
and then well, it's just a friend of a friend or my distant
relative... and by now it's so close that we have to let
these analytical illusions fall and admit, here we are.

Friends, there is no other place. There is no other
group. There is no other.

Yes, let's draw our loved ones close.

All of them.

It's the only thing to do.

*May we be one.*

## APRIL 2020

One of my favorite worlds from divinity school is
"liminality" – it's a word for the betwixt-and-between,
the neither-here-nor-there. The gap between life and
death is liminal space. The pause before the chorus of
*Good Vibrations* is a liminal space.

There are just three rules for liminal space, as far as I can tell.

> First, we're not allowed to stay. Liminal spaces are
> not permanent.

> Second, we can't go backwards. Only through.

> Third, in the liminality, amazing things are possible.

Dear ones, we are in strange times, betwixt and between.
I'm drinking the same coffee, but the beans were
handed to me in a silent parking lot by a shop worker in
gloves and mask. I'm doing the same daily work, but my
colleagues are all pixels instead of people.

Here is the good news, according to the rules above:

> We will exit this liminal state eventually.

> We will go through, not back.

> Right now, in the liminality, we are in a space
> of immense potential.

What do we choose?

In impossible times, impossible things are possible.

*May we have faith.*

## APRIL 2020

It's a curious thing, to be surrounded by people but still separated. Even for a devoted introvert like me, there is a desire to communicate, to see loved ones and greet neighbors and acknowledge strangers as we move through our days.

Perhaps this is what I was missing when I cut out a giant heart to put in my apartment window.

Over the following week a wonderful thing happened. A whole bunch of neighbors from the apartment building across the street put hearts in their windows too. One even put, "Hello!" in big block cut-outs. Now every time I look out the window, I see a flurry of neighborly greetings.

It occurs to me that these neighbors might think I am five years old.

But so what? Aren't we all really still five years old? Life might be easier if I were more patient with my own inner kid. Sometimes, we all need a snack, or a nap, or a hug. Sometimes, we need to jump or sing or dance, or to make a giant paper heart.

Let's look for ways to care for the kids among us – no matter their actual age.

*May we take heart.*

## MAY 2020

I am really not comfortable in the water, especially
water that does not have walls around it. I like to
have my feet on the floor, or my hand on an edge.
Preferably both.

In overcoming this fear, brute force got me the first few
steps. In a chlorinated pool, with whistles and shouts all
around, I managed the essentials of not drowning. But
what got me to finally let go of the edge was curiosity.
Seeing the flash of a sea turtle in the ocean, I wanted
so badly to follow it that without even thinking, I
started to swim.

We are so good at fear, rooted to the floors and
holding tight to the edges.
And we are so good at fighting, with plans and
data and language of war.
Those might serve us well, and keep us safe. But they
can only get us so far.

Dear ones, in this time when masking and cleaning and
distancing is smart and needed and quickly becoming
a way of life, we need to most urgently ask,

Where is the turtle?

Where can our curiosity pull us? Where can we let go?
Where can we float free?

Who knows what we might discover when we do.

*May we release.*

## MAY 2020

One of the best rites of spring is the re-emergence of the honeybees. But this year, one of my hives was silent all through the spring.

Knowing that this happens regularly does not make it easy. Determined to recover, I found a local raiser-of-bees, tucked two new hives securely into the back of my car, and started zipping down the Mass Pike.

Then I saw a little bee bouncing against the back window. Then two. Then four. When I arrived home to find a cluster of a thousand bees or so gathered outside the box, my heart sank. In the end, it all worked out, but not at all as originally expected.

Sometimes our plans go awry. And sometimes the backup plan does not go so well either. Often we need a backup to the backup to the backup... at which point it's not a plan at all, it's just adapting and improvising and deep breathing and maybe a tiny dash of panic.

In this upside-down time, when all of our beautiful plans might be flying loose and in danger of being lost forever, let's welcome the buzzing as best we can, with patience and creativity and care.

If we are lucky, eventually, the honey will follow.

*May we adapt.*

## MAY 2020

When there's a break or a rupture, nature turns towards
the weakness, turns towards the pain.

When our skin is cut, dozens of intricate processes rush
into action. Platelets form a clot to stop the bleeding;
cytokines call out to neutrophils and macrophages,
T-cells send more specialized help, B-cells produce
antibodies. They are fighting against infection, yes. But
it's more than that, better than that. They are fighting
FOR health, for thriving, for life.

Everything turns towards the injury, all hands on deck
to begin the healing process from the inside out. A
bandage on the outside does no good when the
infection is already on the inside.

We have been closed away from the world for weeks,
for months, for lifetimes. We have had a chance to
witness the very best in humanity, and the very worst.
There is a lot of weakness. There are a lot of breaks.

In our pain, it might be tempting to cocoon even further
inward, to turn away. But that's not how nature works.
Nature turns towards the weakness. Nature directs all
resources towards healing.

Friends, we are infected by viruses both literal and
conceptual. A simple bandage will not do. Let's muster
all of our resources. Let's rush to our own defense.

From the inside out.

*May we heal.*

# JUNE 2020

When I first had a patch of ground to plant, I had visions of flowers and fruits and majestic trees and cute little bunnies who never ate the tulips. That first year, I planted a few trees, and quickly turned over a patch of grass to plant some fast-blooming but short-lived annual flowers.

The flowers were immediately stunning. The trees, on the other hand, were just sad-looking sticks.

Fortunately, as time passed, I started listening to people who knew more about this place and this soil and this climate, people who guided me in both the planting and the tending.

Today the little stick-trees are branching way over my head with bounty and splendor. A layer of perennials has formed, steady beauties that return each season. And because the rest is healthy, the annuals are easy, a small simple accent, easy to tend.

For so long we have treated our most serious needs, both individual and collective, as if they are annual flowers, as if quick thoughtless investment should produce stunning and lasting results.

We need to tend the soil.
We need to listen to those who know.
We need to plant every layer with care.

Not just this season, but forevermore.

*May we invest.*

## JUNE 2020

I have been using the language of crisis to describe
our current conditions – health crisis, economic crisis,
environmental crisis, justice crisis – yet this is incomplete.

Intertwined with all of these, there is Hope, the last
creature left in Pandora's jar. And it's not a weak and
fluttery thing.

I see millions of people rising up to care for others,
despite the risks to their own well-being.

I see entrepreneurs creating new solutions for these
changing times, and communities rallying around local
points of exchange.

I see peaceful protest and sold-out books and open-
hearted action and painful reflection and deep listening.

I see skies clearing and gardens sprouting, everywhere.

None of this might have been needed if times
were more ordinary.
None of this might have been possible if times
were more ordinary.

Friends, we are swimming in a sea that can't be seen,
because we're in it. Our arms are tired and our eyes are
stinging and our breath is ragged.

But the winds are shifting.

Who knows what they might bring?

*May we hope.*

✳

*May we be safe.*
*May we be still.*
*May we be one.*
*May we have faith.*
*May we have luck.*
*May we take heart.*
*May we release.*
*May we adapt.*
*May we heal.*
*May we invest.*
*May we hope.*

✳

AUTHOR'S NOTE

# Author's Note

Two great joys in my life are reading and puzzle solving. One of the first worlds I entered by book-traveling as a child, alongside Oz and Whoville and Narnia, was the 1800's prairie land of the United States, thanks to Laura Ingalls Wilder.

In one of those Little House books, a friend was greeted with, "I haven't seen you in a month of Sundays!" ...and here my two joys combined. I still remember my kid-brain struggling to understand this phrase. What was a month of Sundays? Finally I worked out that a this must be a long measure of time, something you'd say to greet a loved one you'd really missed.

Many years later, I started writing short "Sunday Best" posts as part of our work with Honeybee Capital. When the investment parts of Honeybee transformed into my professional role at Putnam, the Sunday posts continued. As my days have happily filled up with more

data and analysis, writing on Sundays has
increasingly become a touchstone for me,
a little pocket of reflection, guaranteed
each week.

In these topsy-turvy times, I find myself turning
back to traveling by book instead of airplane,
to exploring from within, to connecting in spirit
instead of in person.

Dear friends, I haven't seen you in a month of
Sundays! I offer this collection as a greeting for
the people and the places who are missing
right now, and missed. I am delighted to be
able to bundle up this collection for you,
delivered with love.

*Katherine Collins*
*2020*
*Home*

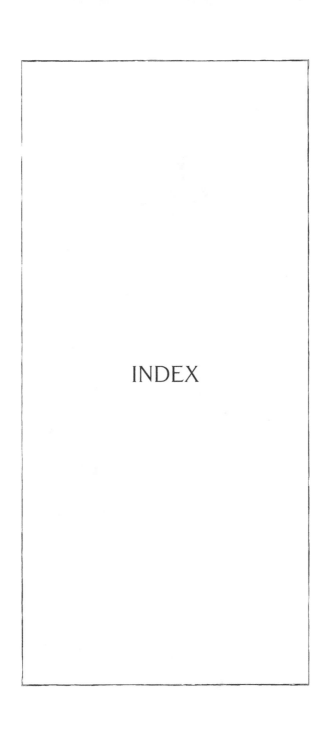

INDEX

001.

I.

II.

III.

IV.

V.

VI.

*Ver*

SPRING

TITLE

002.

*Aestas*

TITLE

003.

I.

II.

III.

IV.

V.

VI.

*Autumnus*

AUTUMN

TITLE

004.

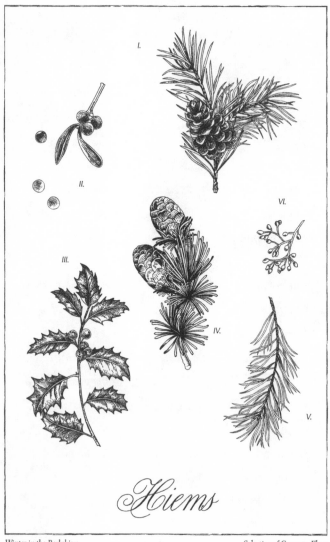

*Hiems*

WINTER

TITLE

ACKNOWLEDGMENTS

# Acknowledgments

As always, a huge spiral of gratitude is owed to all who contributed to bringing this book into being.

Shalon Ironroad has been my steadfast right-hand person for all things Honeybee, a rare being who combines stellar technical skills with deep wisdom and caring and insight.

Christa Alexandra Designs created the incredible visual imagery on these pages, a perfect blend of beauty and whimsy and meaning.

Anna Higgins served as the youngest design editor in history, with a wonderful mix of discernment, conviction, and enthusiasm.

Beyond these specific contributions lies the vibrant community that surrounds me, and supports my whole life and work in the world. My colleagues near and far are a constant source of inspiration and gratitude. My friends are a constant source of comfort and joy.

Being born into my family remains the greatest good fortune of my very lucky life, and being able to learn from a place where the maples grow and the bees buzz and the great black bear occasionally visits for breakfast is a tremendous blessing indeed.

For all of this, I am grateful.

Please stay in touch with our ongoing
Sunday Best publications at
Honeybee Capital Foundation

www.honeybeecapital.org

CPSIA information can be obtained
at www.ICGtesting.com
Printed in the USA
BVHW031255171220
595870BV00004B/25